# DESERT STORM
## A BRIEF HISTORY

### BY

### LENARD D. MOORE

*For
Marsha Warren
In Poetry
&
Friendship,
Lenard D. Moore
II
February 28, 1993*

Los Hombres Press

Desert Storm: A Brief History

Cover by Jeff Kronen

Library of Congress Cataloging in Publication Data 92-075363
Desert Storm: A Brief History
ISBN 1-879603-17-9

Printed in the United States of America

First Edition

1 2 3 4 5 6 7 8 9 10

**Los Hombres Press**
Box 632729
San Diego, CA 92163-2729

# Acknowledgments

I want to thank the following people for telling and retelling their war stories: my father, Rogers Edward Moore, and my brother, Edward Jerome Moore. I am greatly indebted to a photograph taken by Rhonda Collins's cousin who served in the Persian Gulf War, and to the questions raised by E. Ethelbert Miller about this poem. Surprised thanks are due to Joe Nutt, Nina Wicker, Vincent Tripi, and Alexis Rotella for their encouragement of this particular work.

I especially want to thank, too, the individuals who read this poem in manuscript: Lorraine Ellis Harr, Cor van den Heuvel, Rebecca Rust, and Elizabeth Searle Lamb.

"first pilot rescued," "flashlight turned off," and "a young infantryman" were first published in *Modern Haiku.* "moon shadows" was first published in *Frogpond.* "September sunrise," and "quiet night" were first published in *The Griot.* "nightfall," "after the desert sortie," and "Iraqi sunrise," which was originally "dusty sunrise" first appeared in *Black Bear Review.* "a black soldier" was first published in the anthology, *The Gulf Within* (Two Autumns Press, 1991). "Desert Storm," and "rising March sun" were first published in *Portraits Poetry Magazine.*

# Author's Note

In this book I hope to share insights about a specific event with the reader while showing a relationship between history and literature. I choose the haiku form to present the images in a precise way, so that the reader can participate in the haiku moment itself. Here are the sounds and silences of the Persian Gulf War. While the poems can stand independently, it is hoped that this sequence will be read as one long poem. Perhaps the poem will trigger familiar thoughts based on the reader's own experiences. Then, too, I have tried to paint a picture that will inspire a full appreciation of such a global event. This event began on January 17, 1991, a bittersweet day: sweet in the respect that it was my paternal grandmother's 76th birthday, and bitter in the respect that my brother and others had to face the harsh realities of war.

Lenard D. Moore
Raleigh, North Carolina, USA
Summer 1991

# Introduction

## Narratives of Time and Temperature

Reviewing Lenard D. Moore's first book, *The Open Eye,* several years ago, I felt it important to observe that he is representative of a new breed of African-American poet, writers who take their artistic freedom literally and literarily, appropriating whatever they deem germane from the pool of possibility. The best of them are inventive within a tradition or in cross-fertilizing traditions. Their work is vigorous and infused with *difference.* Moore has always been confident in his experimentations with Oriental form and African-American cultural imperatives. Like Spike Lee, he is willing to risk the cutting edge. His success in writing haiku has been a rewarding gesture of liberation and of discipline. And *Desert Storm: A Brief History* is proof that haiku can be domesticated.

This poetic chronicle of the Persian Gulf War that began on January 17, 1991, may trigger recollections of Issa's Oraga *Haru* or the *Year of My Life* (1819) for haiku scholars, only Moore's book of haibun leaves the prose invisible so as to underscore the postmodern extremities of military ventures and our representation/reception of them. This book is a narrative of time from

September sunrise
Marine leaving for Persian Gulf
looks back at his wife

to

welcome home parade
between sun and parting clouds
sky of confetti

and a narrative of temperature, in the sense that the natural and the induced heat and cold of the desert scene may correspond to our passionate convictions about the political morality of modern warfare.

Unlike a sonnet sequence which does not tell a story, Moore's haiku sequence is employed as a chronology of American civilian and military emotions during the drama of "freeing" Kuwait and "disempowering" Iraq. The poet's announced intention is to use haiku to give us precise images, "the sounds and silences of the Persian Gulf War." To achieve this end, Moore violates certain structural principles of classical haiku, the result being poetic forms closer to imagism. Thus the associational narrative challenges readers to meditate on televised warfare and the human meaning of

a black soldier
breathing into a saxophone
hot desert wind

and

a lady private
polishing-up her brass
blessing of warm rain

The accumulated images which mark the space and time of narrative force readers to write the prose that is the real brief history of Desert Storm: the complex fears, griefs, racial speculations, uncertainties, anger, provocatively gendered roles, and stress that dominated public thought in the States and on the sites of battle. Desert Storm: A Brief History allows each reader to construct a different story.

Moore exploits the visual and emotional potential of haiku in this long poem. He lays bare one of the problematics of history, the struggle for persuasive narrative explanation. The haiku or data are overtly subjective. They invite us to create narratives, many of them conflicting with one another. Everything, as William Carlos Williams noticed many years ago, depends on placement, our interest-laden perspectives. Moore has done well in discovering contemporary uses for ancient forms.

Reading *Desert Storm: A Brief History* is like playing a very sophisticated game. The pleasure is not in winning. It exists in the skill we have in constructing, to borrow Sterling D. Plumpp's phrase, "the story always untold." Or, as Gwendolyn Brooks wrote, "For having first to civilize a space / Wherein to play your violin with grace." There is profit in reading and rereading Moore's poem, for each passage through *Desert Storm* is truly a different story.

Jerry W. Ward, Jr.
Tougaloo College
July 17, 1991

For my father,

Rogers Edward Moore, GySgt (ret)

who served in the Vietnam War;

for my brother,

Edward Jerome Moore, SSG

who served in the Persian Gulf War;

and for all the other veterans

who served in previous wars

September sunrise
Marine leaving for the Persian Gulf
looks back at his wife




the reporter says,
"Iraqi tanks roll into Kuwait"
            rousing the president




the phone call to leave
a tear rolls off mother's face
into the warm light




from snapping beans
brother's wife moves swiftly
the TV anchorman

"daddy where you going?"
his daughter stomps again
elm leaves dripping


in last night's dream
a crow lights on a pine bough—
he leaves for the Gulf


a squad of soldiers
boarding the wet cattlecar
none smiling

the rainwet GI
who refused to go to the Gulf—
his handcuffs glisten

army engineers
bulldozing a wall of sand
the heat progresses


desert wind
into a bright cloud of sand
a tank U-turns


a pair of jump boots
left at the tent's entrance
the hot dawn light

woman at the P.O.
mailing the package marked Kuwait
shadows on her face

briefing the troops
general with his helmet off
in the drilling sun


tent shadows
touch the soldier on guard
singing to himself


dust drifts
where the duffle bags were
the white-hot sun


beyond the tent
and the dark sky's silence
a soldier's cough


6

a yellow ribbon
around the schoolyard oak
in morning fog

before dawn's heat
a young soldier shaving
in a mud puddle


mail call
red print of his wife's kiss
smeared in the heat

a lady private
polishing-up her brass
blessing of warm rain




high noon
the dark columns
of tank tracks




a grenade explodes
shadows of soldiers skirting
the desert road

sun submerges
in billowing oil smoke
flashes of land mines


after the desert sortie
an airman takes a deep breath
of airless heat


a tank idles
september moon rising
hot sand blowing


bomb after bomb
smoking up the night desert
the cries of soldiers

Desert Shield night
once again machine guns
in the distance




a black soldier
breathing into a saxophone
hot desert wind

flag sticker
peeling off her windshield
the midday heat

marine tanks lining up
at a single fuel depot
desert crosswinds


black clouds rising
from the ammo dump
a wild dog barks


a tank buried
behind a wall of sand
the soldier's watch ticks


two sweaty GIs
stacking sandbags in a trench
faroff bombs

Iraqi soldiers
still sitting in their bunkers
evening silence


glinting there
in the desert sands
the sergeant's dog tags


shadowy moonlight
a bullet-hit canteen
leaking in the sand

quiet night
eyes of a soldier shining
in the shadows


warm burst of rain—
a woman marine at daybreak
drawing in the sand

Iraqi soldiers
shuffling toward stacked weapons
the glowing sun


charcoal smoke lifting
over the downed fighter plane
the burning sun


the missile pierces
a bed of unmoving clouds
its sunglint sound


a dead soldier
staring from the ground
the shifting light

a lone GI
slowly nears an abandoned jeep
onrush of stars




the corporal
shouting into the radio
star-blistered sky

midday heat
soldiers on both sides
roll up their sleeves


Red Cross nurse
entering the latrine
gusts of hot wind


acre after acre
of scorched Iraqi tanks
the haze of battle

a wild dog
nosing the dead soldier's hand—
faint hint of stench


mortar launched—
sandpile becomes a crater
sucking hot air


B-52 bomber
releasing cluster bombs
distant thunder

distant flares
lighting up the sky
hunkered shapes of black


moonless desert
the mine sweeper sweeping
hour after hour


shimmering heat waves—
behind the truck's steering wheel
a charred corpse


helmet deep in sand
the soldiers stop before
moving black shapes

night heat
the blown-off arm
still in fatigues




a line of soldiers
waiting in the night's hush
smell of scorched earth

August noon sun
layers of dust rise upward
another air alert

white soldier crawling
on muddy elbows and knees
a clatter of weapons


two black soldiers
reaffirming their patriotism
thunder and lightning

in white t-shirts
soldiers jogging at sundown
roadside maples' shade

a woman marine
gazing into the jeep's mirror
the hot dusk




the heat deepens
platoon's keg of water
darkens with each drop




one hundredth hour
the last soldier's gun goes silent
the hot smoke

Sunday morning
a black GI prays
inside his tent

cleaning his weapon
a soldier with the hot sun
setting in his eyes

"stack plenty sandbags
in the bunker," father says
breathing into the phone

shimmering sun
drying the GI's blood
into the sand


beside the cargo
a private turns his gas mask
toward the full moon


nightfall
a battleship wavers the moon
on the oil slick

distant notes of taps
last flicker of light grows dim
on the shipping port




artillery rounds
growing louder and louder
in winter dusk

blood-stained shirt
on a wounded soldier
rising desert moon


first light
a bombed-out jeep smoking
in desert silence


young chaplain
closing the eyes
of a dead soldier


a young infantryman
closing his eyes
to every dead soldier

sun's last glimmer
beyond the oil platform
the tanker's smoke


flashlight turned off
a GI wiping the stars
on his mess kit


rainy night
the jeep's tires sinking in
at the ammo dump

his letter home
sand from Saudi Arabia
glistening in it

Iraqi sunrise
through windows of a waiting bus
dirty-face soldiers


soldiers running
along the barb-wired border
moonless night


heat-wind at sunrise
the rocket gunner's yawn
still too dark

desert afternoon
at a field telephone
troops lined up



after the skirmish
a rag-tag band of soldiers
raising our flag



after the sound
of a battleship's guns
deadly silence

warm evening
awaiting the names of the dead
the quiet voices




soldier's sweaty face
on *Time's* glossy cover
the grin

quiet dusk
a Scud missile strikes
the barracks


dawn's first run
blood leaks from a body bag
in the helicopter


desert heat
a camel pokes its head
into the foxhole

first pilot rescued
twirling helicopter blades
between earth and stars




blowing sand
enters the tank's ruins—
quiet after battle

a GI watches
camel shadows lengthening
in dusky light




airborne troops
jogging into the dawn light
camels sleeping

mortar fire—
three soldiers wounded
in a Red Cross van

the squeaking boots
of rain-soaked soldiers
camel's silent pace

wet desert sand
soldier after soldier plodding
in others' footprints



a wounded soldier
lying by a blasted tent
full moon in his eyes

dawn's crescent moon
the missileman raises
the launcher


another Patriot
rises to meet the Scud—
the smell of a latrine


waving torn white flags
a line of Iraqi men—
the first hush of guns

waves of desert heat—
privates handing out M.R.E.
beside the nearest palm


Top Guns catapulting
into the sun's gold glare
soldiers hunkered down


rising March sun
lights up tent after tent
in desert silence

desert wind all day
and with it the roar
of fighter jets



camel caravan
the air raid siren sounds again
brilliant sunset

oil well fires
clouds of black smoke drifting
over desert sun


alone in his tent
black GI's clasped hands
in a shaft of moon


Desert Storm
deep warmth of the tank's
starlit barrel

December 25th
a stealth fighter crosses
the desert sun

another sunrise
without weapons or canteens
cooks' platoon

moon shadows
soldiers in camouflage
taking cover

sand rises and falls
back on the same dune
a GI sweating


dust storm
a helicopter crashes
into a sand dune


March 17—
shell casings still pale
in the moonrise


unshaven GI
watches the camel's lips moving
in the moonlight

3 A.M.
brother's voice on the phone
in a different tone

crescent moon
aircraft carrier awaiting
each bomber's return




night firing Patriot
middle-aged chaplain patting
young soldier's back

sick call
silence of a pale GI
in humid dawnlight


one hundredth day
Red Cross ship flaming
where the sun rose


oil-slicked sea
sailor peers into the sun's
white heat

an American soldier
checking the Kuwaiti woman's ID
rain-swishing traffic




empty bucket on her head
a woman walks to the Euphrates
in acid rain




chill of evening
a low-flying plane drops food
to a camp of Kurds

desert photographs
taped inside his wall locker
rain pelting the window


humid night
Desert Storm postage stamp
curling in her hand

bulldozers pushing
corpses into the deep hole
another dawn




the mines all cleared
where brilliant light hits the beach
only the sand moves

welcome home parade
between sun and parting clouds
sky of confetti

no one waving
at the passing hearse
noonlit leafbuds

the open grave—
his mother's pale hands tremble
with the folded flag


21 gun salute
soft wind and rain falling
at the gravesite


the flag drapes
his dove-grey coffin
the silence


warm gusts—
she sets up the wreath again
on her son's grave

back home
soldier listens to birdcalls
marking sunrise

# Afterword

It may seem strange, even foolhardy, at first, to find a poet treating a subject as complex and unwieldy as even a brief war with one of the smallest of forms, the baiker. Most of us would have expected a single and larger form—an ode, say, or a double sestina, or un-numbered pages of heroic quatrains.

Then we may remember that a motion picture is made up of thousands of individual pictures that flow into our nervous system as one continual story. It is the nervous system also that, after a while, can take such small poems in as parts of a seamless whole, as if—to shift the metaphor (but not very far)—one were walking invisible across the sands where the siege called Desert Storm took place, looking at the thousands of scenes that finally merge into one. So what we have here is a kind of naturalistic movie. If we want to give it a title, we can call it "Insight."

Miller Williams

# About the Author

Lenard D. Moore was born in Jacksonville, North Carolina, in 1958 and was educated at Coastal Carolina Community College, the University of Maryland, and North Carolina State University. He is a Literary Consultant of the Humanities Extension OUTREACH Program for North Carolina State University, Writer-in-Residence for the United Arts Council of Raleigh and Wake County, and he works for the School Television section in the Division of Media and Technology Services at the North Carolina Department of Public Instruction. From 1978 to 1981, he served in the United States Army. In 1983, he served as Poet-in-Residence at the Mira Mesa Branch Library in San Diego. He has served as associate editor of *Pine Needles,* and staff reviewer of *Library Journal.* He is the author of a chapbook, *Poems of Love And Understanding,* a limited edition, The *Open Eye,* a booklet, *Poems For Performance,* and *Forever Home* (St. Andrews Press). In addition to an Emerging Artist Grant form the City of Raleigh Arts Commission, Lenard D. Moore's awards include the Haiku Museum of Tokyo Award, Outstanding Young Man of America awards, a Pushcart Prize Nomination, a General Electric Foundation Award for Younger Writers Nomination, and a Lamont Poetry Prize Nomination. He is a member of The National Book Critics Circle. *Desert Storm: A Brief History* is Lenard D. Moore's second full-length collection of poetry. He lives in Raleigh, North Carolina, with his wife, Lynn, and daughter, Maiisha.